CONTENTS

C000043442

Edited by John Gent and Isabel MacLeod

Published by The Old Croydonians' Association

ISBN 0-9548783-0-2

Printed by DAP (Sussex) Ltd

48 pages   54 illustrations

INTRODUCTION

This booklet celebrates the centenary of the foundation of the Selhurst Schools in 1904. Hitherto, nothing has been published about the school first known as the Croydon Borough School for Girls, then Selhurst Grammar School for Girls, and latterly Selhurst High School for Girls. The Boys' School has fared much better with books published in 1925 and 1954. For this reason, rather more details are included here for the Girls' School, than for the Boys' School, but it is intended to give a brief summary of the history of both establishments and perhaps to encourage the production of a more detailed and scholarly history at sometime in the future.

From the modest beginnings in 1904 until closure in 1988, nearly 12,000 boys and over 11,000 girls received their education at the schools. All benefited from their years at the schools and many made highly successful careers in their chosen vocations. Some became famous, such as Malcolm Muggeridge, Ronald Delderfield, Sylvia Syms and Shirley Cawley.

Both schools were fortunate in their extremely talented and able teachers. Several started their careers at the Boys' School before the First World War and continued to serve it into the 1950s. Some were educated at the school and later returned to teach there. Similarly, some of the girls returned to teach at the school at which they had been educated.

Over the years the schools suffered a number of changes, problems and setbacks but despite these achieved high educational standards. The story culminated in the closure of both schools in 1988. Subsequent developments, the reopening of the Boys' School and the use of the Girls' School as a Performing Arts Centre have resulted in both buildings remaining in use, in modified form, over 90 years after their construction. Long may they continue to fulfil, in different circumstances, their educational purpose.

EARLY DAYS TO 1914

The recommendations of the 1895 Bryce Commission on Secondary Education led to the 1902 Education Act. Within ten years the County and County Borough Council had founded 330 new secondary schools and had taken over 53 existing ones.

Croydon Council set up an Education Committee to replace the former Croydon School Board. In 1903 the Committee decided to have secondary schools for boys and girls. Originally it was suggested that the schools should be co-educational but the Committee decided against this. The most urgent requirement was the provision of better educational facilities for the pupil teachers. These were young people between the ages of fourteen and eighteen who were attempting the task of combining the teaching of others with their own education! The Pupil Teachers' Centre at Whitehorse Road School was conducted in part by Mr Arthur Hillyer. In Croydon as in most other places, the pupil teachers were at the centre for two or three half-days a week and were teaching for the other seven or eight. From the centre they passed to a training college and then back to the elementary schools they had left so recently.

The boys and girls from this centre became the first scholars of the Borough Secondary Schools. In September 1904 the boys were transferred to the Central Polytechnic in Scarbrook Road and the girls to South

1. This 1904 photograph shows the pupil teachers at the Whitehorse Road Centre. Most of them would probably have gone on to the new Borough Schools to complete their education and were thus some of the first pupils. Mr Arthur Hillyer, (front row – eighth from left) was principal of the Pupil Teachers' Centre from its inception in 1889 until 1904. He then became first Headmaster of the Borough School for Boys. He retired from Selhurst in 1920 and moved to Wickford in Essex where he founded an electricity supply company for the village. He died in 1938 at the age of 82 and was cremated at Croydon.

Norwood Polytechnic in Selhurst Road. In July of that year the Education Committee had recommended that they be authorised to negotiate with the Whitgift Governors for the acquisition of a site in The Crescent, Selhurst. The site, described as rough bogland, would have to be drained and levelled before building could begin.

Croydon Borough School for Boys

The school was opened on 15th September 1904 by the Mayor, Alderman Harold Morland. Mr Arthur Hillyer B.A. became the first Headmaster and the Assistant Masters were Messrs S Chambers B.A: Mathematics; W D Ferguson M.A: French; H R Rogers B.A: Science; H A Treble M.A: English and Latin; and H Drew R.B.A: Drawing. By 1906 Messrs W H Bentley, M.A: A R Headland, B.A., BSc: and F T B Wheeler, M.A. had joined the staff.

There were 63 pupils on the roll and four forms. The number of pupils increased to 153 by 1906. For the first three years the fees were £2 a term but in 1907 a free-place system was introduced for a quarter of the boys. The fees had risen to £5 a term by the time they were abolished as a result of the 1944 Education Act.

The Central Polytechnic building was far from convenient and quite unsuited to scholastic needs. Mr Bentley (Headmaster from 1920 to 1939) recalled that it "was next door to the County Court and was a distinct threat to the peace of mind of the somewhat irascible Registrar, Major Fox, who occasionally found it necessary or expedient to send in a peremptory warning that the court was in session and he could not hear himself speak during our play interval".

In 1925, A T Law, a pupil from 1907 to 1912, recalled the early days. "Yet how we loved, in our own way, those straggling buildings at Scarbrook Hill, every nook and corner of which we knew so well. What advantages they had from our point of view! Long,

dimly lit corridors and dark passages that gave us every opportunity for sport – sport of the mischievous kind, beloved of the schoolboy fraternity! Think of the north staircase with its long and polished rails, providing a rapid, exhilarating but forbidden mode of descent! How many pairs of trousers came there to an untimely end, or at least had their useful life curtailed!".

School sports started with football but there was no field. One description of a ground used by the team is that "it was full of ruts, covered with bricks, and with grass about six inches long". Cricket too was played from the beginning on waste patches around the town, and later, by permit on local recreation grounds. Athletic sports were held first in a field belonging to the Croydon Gas Company, then at Mitcham on the railway sports ground, and subsequently at the school playing field, opened at The Crescent in 1909, and described as "a wild and thorny heath adorned with holes".

A school magazine was first published in the Spring Term of 1906 and continued on a fairly regular basis until the 1980s.

Mr Bentley recalled in 1954 that the teaching of Science in the Polytechnic building was difficult. Chemistry was possible as the school was permitted to use the laboratory, but physics was more or less limited to the subjects of heat, light and sound. The subject of Biology was more or less "on the secret list" and was scarcely considered a suitable subject of study for young boys, except perhaps those wishing to become doctors.

In September 1907 the Board of Education gave notice to Croydon Corporation that recognition of the school would be discontinued unless within twelve months there were definite proposals for the removal of the school to a site and building elsewhere. In 1909 the Council at last decided to proceed with the building of a new school on the site at The Crescent, by which time the new building for the Girls'

School was almost complete.

However, it was not until 15th October 1913 that the new building was opened by the Mayor of Croydon, Councillor S Rogers in the presence of a large gathering representing every aspect of public life in the town. Among the guests was Mr Cyril Cobb, the Chairman of the London County Council who congratulated the school on its new building (which became the prototype of a number built by the L.C.C. in the following years). The building was designed by Mr H Carter Pegg FRIBA. It cost £14,493, and the entire furnishing cost £1,200. Accommodation was provided for 414 pupils. There were chemistry and physics laboratories, workshop with dining room for 100 above, and a gymnasium.

Removal to the new buildings was a convenient time to introduce the house system. It was intended that the number of houses should be increased to six and possibly more as soon as the number of boys justified this. Temporary names were taken from the first four letters of the Greek alphabet. The names and house colours remained unchanged throughout the life of the school – Alpha = red; Beta = green; Gamma = blue and Delta = yellow. Apparently dreadful school ties were introduced at the same time with half-inch horizontal stripes of white and the house colour. It is not known when these were replaced by more conventional items.

Croydon Borough School for Girls

There is only a little documentary evidence of the first few years of the Girls' School's existence. The first Head Mistress was Jane E Holden, appointed with effect from 1st September 1904. A mystery shrouds Jane Holden's tenure of the post, as it appears from the Croydon Education Committee Minutes for the period between the months of January and March, 1906 that Miss Holden was asked to resign. It is hoped that further research may be able to reveal more details of the circumstances which brought this about, and also more information about Jane Holden herself.

Edith Wohlmann was appointed the second Head Mistress with effect from 1st September 1906. Born in 1874 in Hertford, she had gained a BA from Royal Holloway College, having previously sat the Oxford Honours Moderations in Mathematics. Her career before her arrival at Selhurst was via schools in Devonport and Walsall, where she had been Assistant First Mistress at Queen Mary's School. Aged only thirty-three, Edith Wohlmann took on the responsibility of ensuring that the new school would not only be a success, but also supervised its removal to the new premises. The Croydon Borough School for Girls moved to Selhurst in 1909.

The first pupils of the school in South Norwood had been enrolled in 1904 – only fifty-six of them in what appear to have been three classes. They were not all eleven year olds, as some entered in different forms or 'levels'. Of those fifty-six girls who entered the Croydon Borough Girls' School in the autumn of 1904, it appears that they came from a variety of previous schools and a variety of social backgrounds. They came from approximately twenty-four previous schools, of which fifteen were Elementary Schools, five Private Schools, three Secondary Schools (Coloma, Old Palace and Croydon High School) and one an LCC Higher Grade Mixed School. The largest single group came from Beulah Road School in Thornton Heath (7), followed by Woodside Girls' (5). Other than that they were from various parts of the Borough, although the majority lived in the Thornton Heath and South Norwood areas. A few travelled a longer distance each day from either South Croydon in the south of the Borough, or Streatham, which was to the north and outside the Borough.

From the admissions registers it is possible

2. The Croydon Polytechnic Building in Scarbrook Road, photographed in about 1955. This was the first home of the Croydon Borough School for Boys from 1904 until 1913, and again from 1915 until 1919. Although considered unsuitable for school purposes even in 1904 it was used for a third time for the juniors of Selhurst Grammar School from 1958 until 1965. The buildings were demolished in the 1960s.

to piece together miniature biographies of some of the girls. The early records are both beautifully preserved and presented. Apart from the details to be expected, such as name, address and date of birth, the occupation of the parent or guardian is included. In most cases, it is details of the fathers which are listed, but for some it is the mother who was the breadwinner. In most cases there are details of terms kept by the girls, examinations sat and also their destination on leaving school. Many took up formal teacher's training, with about half of the first intake going to Goldsmiths College, and a further nine to St Gabriel's College[1]. Some moved into either commerce or shop

[1] *A Church of England Training College later merged with Goldsmith's College.*

work: others simply stayed at home. One individual went to Gymnastic College.

These girls were all at school together, receiving an identical education irrespective of their social class or background. About half were described as being Pupil Teachers at the school, and the other half Bursars.

At the opening ceremony in South Norwood the Chairman of the Education Committee, Dr John Newnham, told those present that they had been invited to participate in the opening of one of the first institutions of its kind in England. It seems that he meant by this that 40% of the anticipated 350 pupils would hold free places, whilst all other girls' schools in Croydon charged fees in excess of 6 guineas per annum for the tuition of one person.

The early Staff Registers reveal that a well-

qualified selection of teachers was appointed. It seems that subjects were gradually added to the available curriculum. Teachers of French, English, Art, Mathematics, History and Scripture, and Physics were amongst the early staff appointments in 1904. Over the next few years Gymnastics, Science (Chemistry), Singing and Geography (apparently together) and Needlework were added. It must be remembered that as the school was attached to the South Norwood Polytechnic there was probably some flexibility in the first few terms, enabling staff either to be shared or subjects to be introduced gradually for selected pupils.

The information listed for each of the teachers appointed includes personal details such as date of birth and qualifications; it lists the educational establishments attended and any teaching posts previously held. It does not, interestingly, mention marital

3. Girls' School Staff 1911. At that date there were sixteen members of staff: Misses Appleton, Beardsell, Burgis, Carlisle, H Church, Dunnicliff, Green [later Mrs Dexter], Heslop, Nursey, Wohlmann [Wellman], C Church, Edith Fielding, Hudd, Keeling, Perry and Florence Fielding [sister to Edith]. It is believed that Miss Wellman may be the third from left in the middle row.

status: it is to be assumed that nearly all of the ladies were single. One teacher, however, Mrs Dexter, had joined as a single woman, then married and continued working at the School until her retirement in 1945.

A few examples of the first members of staff include Mabel Beardsell, appointed to teach French, who had attended both the Sorbonne and the University of Rennes; Edith Nursey, teacher of Physics and Nature Study, whose qualifications included awards from South Kensington in Advanced Heat and also Inorganic Chemistry; Marguerite Dunnicliffe who attended Girton College, Cambridge and St Mary's College, Paddington, from which she gained a Diploma in Pedagogy. The first Needlework and Dressmaking teacher, Audrey Lockhart, had attended Cheltenham Ladies' College and Liverpool School of Cookery, by which she had been awarded Diplomas in both Needlework and Dressmaking . She then gained a Board of Education Diploma for

Cookery before coming to the Borough School to impart her considerable skills to the new pupils. It would seem that whilst there she was very busy because she also taught Needlework evening classes at the Croydon Polytechnic. Similarly, the first teacher of Gymnastics, May Appleton, holder of Certificates in Physiology and Hygiene, was described as the "Organiser of Physical Training for Croydon Education Committee" – her annual salary was somewhere in the scale of £100 to £105, and, at the time of her appointment, had the potential to rise to a maximum of £130.

Interestingly, the salary offered to the first Head Mistress was £220 per annum, whereas Mr Hillyer, first Head Master of the Boys' School was paid £300 – for doing the same job.

Tenders were invited for the building of the Girls' School in the Crescent. The Education Committee accepted the second cheapest one, at a proposed cost of £13,405, from B E

Nightingale of Albert Embankment, S.E. Turning again to the pupils, of the 84 new pupils who joined the newly opened building in the Crescent in 1909 at least twenty-four lived in Thornton Heath and twenty-five in South Norwood. The rest travelled from all over the Croydon area, and also from areas which would have involved quite an awkward journey, such as Purley or Beckenham[2]. Awards of 2d for every day had been made available from January 1905 for Scholars and Pupil Teachers at the South Norwood building who lived beyond a penny tram fare journey. It is presumed that this continued once the school removed to its new premises.

Most of the 1909 entrants were aged eleven when they entered the school. Many girls progressed to Goldsmiths College after they left school. Some went into shop work: for example, one became a draper's assistant; another was apprenticed to a photographer. Although education was essentially free, there was at least one girl who, according to her records, had to leave because her father was unable to pay some fees that were due. Once again, however, it seems that the mixture of backgrounds was quite varied. For example, the girl who subsequently became School Captain (1914-15), Constance Marchant, was the daughter of a Coach Builder. She lived at various addresses in central Croydon moving from Edridge Road (111) to Mint Walk and then returning to Edridge Road (74) within her time at the school, and possibly as her father's business either expanded or fluctuated in prosperity.

The future looked very bright but soon the country would be at war and both boys and girls would return to their original premises.

4. Girls' School Building – the road surface is incomplete, the building looks very new [no creeper to soften the contours].

GIRLS SECONDARY SCHOOL, CROYDON. W.H.ROGERS.

[2] Beckenham was in Kent [as it still is]. Purley did not become part of Croydon until 1965.

5. *The Crescent War Hospital – a scene in the Girls' School Hall in January 1918.*

6. *A splendid line up of motor vehicles and wounded soldiers in the Girls' School playground around 1917.*

THE WAR YEARS

When war broke out in 1914, the Girls' School had been at The Crescent for five years and the Boys' School for one year. There was no reason to suppose that the war would affect the schools but in Spring 1915 the War Office requisitioned both school buildings for use as a Military Hospital. The boys returned to the Polytechnic building in Scarbrook Road and the girls to South Norwood Polytechnic. One girl from the second form remembered her form being entrusted with conveying some scientific apparatus back to South Norwood and that:

"people saw small girls carrying pipettes and bunsen burners through the streets"

It was during this period that Edith Wohlmann anglicised her name to Wellman. She was undoubtedly English, but presumably of German descent. Her change of name was no doubt due to the general unpopularity of all things German during the First World War.

It seems that there was no official school uniform, for the girls, at that time, but navy blue tunics and black stockings were worn for gym. These tunics were then adopted as the school's winter uniform. The black stockings were still worn in summer with the dresses described as blue 'trioline'. They came two inches below the knee, but for gym lessons buttoned up on to an extra set of buttons. White straw boaters with a black hat band were worn all year round. The hat band had the Borough coat of arms on the front. By about 1917, however, boaters were considered too old fashioned and were superseded by navy felt hats for winter and panamas for summer. These felt hats, in turn, became shabby and the girls were told to take off the hatband, turn up the brim at the front and fasten it with the badge. The girls obligingly turned up the brims of their hats – but all the way round. As this did not meet with official approval they had to learn how to do it properly in their needlework classes.

The staff and the boys had only just got used to their splendid accommodation at The Crescent and the inferior conditions at Scarbrook Road were not popular. A boy "Food Controller" was appointed for each form. At first regarded as a war-time joke, boys refused to view them seriously, especially when they inspected unwanted sandwiches or enquired after the owners of neglected and very stale buns! However Mr Hillyer soon forced the boys to realise their importance. A School Savings Bank was established. Weekly sums as could be spared were to be exchanged in due course for 5/- War Loan scrip vouchers. Each voucher would bear interest at the rate of five per cent per annum until December 1915, when twenty such vouchers would be exchanged for £5 War Bonds. A bonus of one shilling was given with each bond, and the bonds paid 4½ per cent interest.

The formation of a Cadet Corps had already been discussed and took place in 1915. Commanded by Cadet Major Hillyer, it attained a membership of 160 within a term, and was divided into four platoons on a house basis. Many masters joined the army, and mistresses took their place. News of masters, old boys, friends and

7. A kitchen in The Crescent War Hospital – May 1918.

8. The Massage room in the Boys' School gymnasium – August 1917.

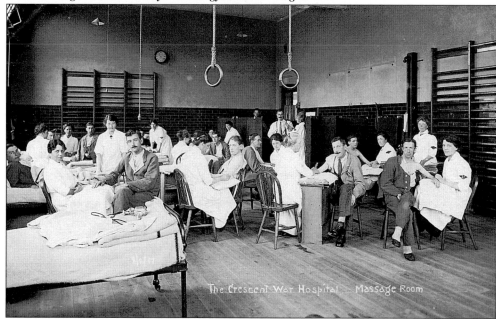

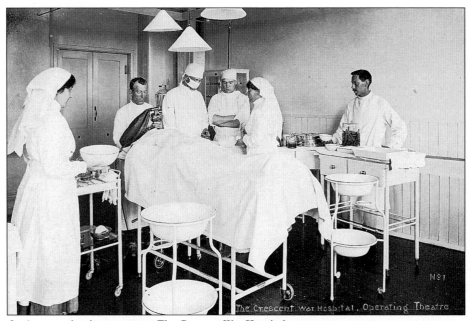

9. *An operation in progress at The Crescent War Hospital.*

relatives who had been wounded or killed, and air raids requiring pupils to dive under their desks for cover, brought home the reality of war.

In Croydon, Davidson Road, Ecclesbourne Road, Ingram Road and Stanford Road Council Schools were requisitioned as war hospitals in a similar way to Selhurst. The total number of hospital beds provided as a result was one thousand. The first patients were admitted on 30th June 1915 and over 19,000 patients were treated at the six schools. It was recorded that a Mrs Edgelow shaved and cut the hair of patients 42,000 times at The Crescent War Hospital!

The school buildings ceased to be used as a hospital soon after the end of the war. The Selhurst schools returned home in time for the Spring term of 1919. For some years afterwards a few of the patients would return to look at the place where they had been nursed back to health following wartime injuries, and both buildings retained evidence of their wartime use.

10. *There was a rapid increase in the number of cadet corps during the First World War. Four companies were formed at the Borough School in 1915, under the overall command of Cadet Major Arthur Hillyer. This unit was designated the 1st Cadet Battalion The Queen's (Royal West Surrey Regiment). This photograph shows some of the first cadets of the Borough School in 1915.*
The School cadet corps flourished until the 1970s.

11. *Whitehorse Road, looking towards Thornton Heath in 1923. One of the shops on the right was used as a Salvage Shop during the Second World War. Boys from the school would collect a barrow on Saturday mornings and collect salvage, in aid of the war effort, from houses and shops in adjacent roads.*

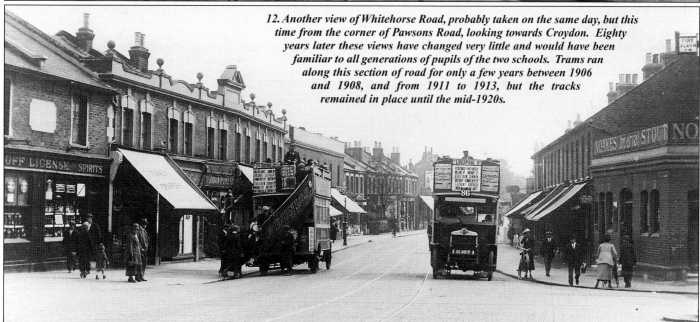

12. *Another view of Whitehorse Road, probably taken on the same day, but this time from the corner of Pawsons Road, looking towards Croydon. Eighty years later these views have changed very little and would have been familiar to all generations of pupils of the two schools. Trams ran along this section of road for only a few years between 1906 and 1908, and from 1911 to 1913, but the tracks remained in place until the mid-1920s.*

13. Selhurst Grammar School for Boys as it appeared in the early 1920s, with the Girls' School beyond.

THE BOYS' SCHOOL – 1919 to 1945

The return of the school to The Crescent in 1919 was followed by twenty years of progress and reasonable stability. Mr Arthur Hillyer, although long past the age of retirement, remained in post to oversee the move and did not retire until the end of the Summer Term of 1920. He was succeeded by Mr Walter H Bentley who had been Second Master and Senior Science Master since 1905.

The years following the First World War were marked by far-reaching changes in the aims and scope of grammar school curricula. The establishment of the VIth forms at this time contributed to many old boys having very distinguished careers.

From the Autumn Term of 1922 the Borough School became Selhurst Grammar School. There was a remarkable stability of staff during this period under the leadership of Mr

H A Treble as Second Master. The few changes there were mostly arose from masters leaving to take up more important work.

There was a great wealth of out-of-school activities. The Hobbies Exhibition, started in 1921, became an annual event and attracted the interest of the national press. Models of all kinds, pieces of scientific apparatus, drawings, paintings, photographs and stamp

14. A classroom in the Boys' School in the early 1920s.

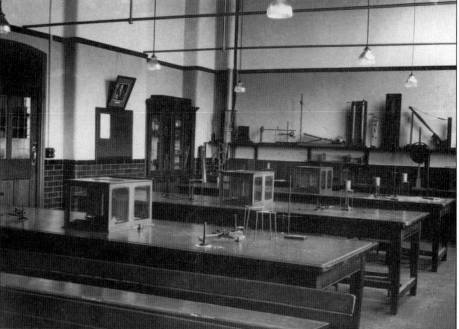

collections vied with cakes and other comestibles made by the boys. The Ludi Literarii, school plays, and the school journeys led by Mr K M King to the French Alps, Belgium and Spain all contributed to the variety of experiences the boys could enjoy.

By 1920 there were 475 boys in the school and by 1925 this had increased to 550. The accommodation was modified in various ways and in the late 1930s a new handicrafts building was opened. There was also a new building for the girls' school with a gymnasium used, not at the same time, by both boys and girls. The doors on the appropriate side were always kept firmly locked to ensure segregation by sex, and there was an invisible wall between the two schools through which neither side was allowed to stray!

In 1933 Mr C W Scott composed the school song, Io Selhurst, with music to Latin words by Dr J A Wright. Mr Scott later wrote "the music came to me while I was riding into Croydon on top of a 68 bus". A few years later, in 1936, the school organ was built by the boys under supervision. The inaugural concert was given by Dr George Thalben-Ball.

Sporting activities continued to be important and in the summer of 1939 Selhurst was the champion grammar school in Surrey for swimming.

15 & 16. *Two pictures of laboratories in the Boys' School in the early 1920s.*

Above right: **17.** *The Science Corridor on the first floor of the Boys' School in the early 1920s.*

Right: **18.** *This photograph shows a Prize-Giving in the School Hall in the 1920s. Captain J Stevenson, Chairman of the Governors is on the extreme left, and Mr Bentley (Headmaster) is on the right.*

19. The School Hall in the 1920s. This could accommodate all the boys in the school for morning assembly. A temporary, larger stage could be erected for dramatic productions, concerts etc. After the closure of the school in 1988 a mezzanine floor was built and the area has since been sub-divided into smaller rooms.

Mr Walter Bentley retired at the end of the Summer Term, 1939, and his successor, Mr Frederick W Turner M.A. took over at a very inauspicious time. He first met the staff officially on 3rd September 1939 in order to arrange for the evacuation on the following day! The school too had assembled for instructions about the evacuation which took place on Monday 4th September. The school ended up in Hove and eventually shared accommodation with Brighton and Hove Grammar School. They used the building in the morning and Selhurst used it from 2 to 6pm, working six periods of 35 to 40 minutes each. As the "phoney war" continued with little threat of air raids, some boys returned to Croydon and it was necessary to reopen the school in The Crescent for a limited number of pupils. About 200 boys attended, with a staff of eight. The Sixth Form could not be accommodated so they went to Whitgift Middle School. Several masters and mistresses spent part of their time in Hove and part in Croydon, running a "mixed school". Following the collapse of France in June 1940, the South coast was in direct line of attack, and the school was removed to Bideford in North Devon. Only about 180 boys went there and at the end of July 1942, the raids having died down for the time being, the school was reunited in Croydon for the Autumn Term.

More air-raid shelters were needed and brick and concrete structures were put up in the playground. These were lighted only by candles and work in them was difficult to say the least. There were Salvage and National Savings drives in which the boys took part. The last period on Friday afternoon was designated a "Society" period so that these interests could be maintained without boys

20. A group of boys photographed at the School Sports' Day around 1928. This shows the school uniform and also, judging from their expressions, that one or two boys apparently either disliked being photographed or being at the sports!

21. The teaching staff on the hall platform in 1925. Back row from left to right are; G H Vallins; C J T Clifton; J E C Robinson; A J Barlow; E W King; G W Bosustow; -Long; Miss E M Cayford (School Secretary); Rev P E Hughes; H A Parkinson; J C Wedd; K M King; C W Scott; and A W Pritchard. Front row from left to right are; A R Headland; F Hollinrake; J Katz; F T B Wheeler; H A Treble; W H Bentley (Headmaster); W D Ferguson; S Chambers; H Drew; J A Wright; J A Stevenson. A comparison with illustration 38 on page 33 shows that eight of these masters were still teaching in the school in 1954!

having to stay after school. Sometimes, on the last day of term the whole school would instead assemble in the hall for community singing and an abiding memory is of Mr Bosustow, with a benevolent expression on his face, conducting the assembled multitude in a lusty rendition of "My bonny lies over the ocean". In the middle of June 1944 the attacks by V1s, or "doodle bugs" totally disrupted school activities. Sadly, Mrs Marion Ashton, a temporary member of staff, was killed by one which fell in Saxon Road. The school and the homes of many members of staff and boys received severe damage and many families left the area, so that by the end of the Summer Term only about twenty-five per cent of the possible attendance was registered.

By the beginning of the new school year the threat of air attacks was almost over and the school was able to function almost normally. Out-of-school activities, sports and athletics resumed and the war would soon be over.

22 & 23. In these two photographs dating from about 1943, the Head Master, Mr F W Turner and the School caretaker, Mr Harding assist a group of boys in digging up the lawns in front of the school. Vegetable plots were to be provided in aid of the war effort. The resulting efforts met with a limited degree of success but some boys got a great deal of satisfaction from obtaining water by means of a hosepipe, not always directed at the vegetables.

THE GIRLS' SCHOOL – 1919 to 1945

Back in The Crescent once more, life settled down for a new generation of girls. The building was now provided with two laboratories and a gym[1]. It was seemingly quite sparsely equipped, as would have befitted the exercise permitted to young ladies at that time. There were ropes for climbing, but no wall bars. In fact, the rope hooks, which were never removed, were eyed suspiciously by later generations of girls not always aware of the previous use to which that particular room had been put.

By 1921 the First and Second Forms were in single forms, sorted by date of birth. Higher up the school there was a 'Remove'. This class did Cookery, which was not done in any other form. Singing lessons started in 1921. They took place in a hut in the grounds. It is not clear whether this was as a result of an accommodation problem, or because the participants were especially untuneful. German was not taken at all until 1935 when it was always an alternative to Latin from the Third Year upwards. Biology was introduced as late as 1937.

Of the new teachers appointed at about this time, some were to stay for many years. Enid Fryer joined as a part-time Gymnastics teacher in 1918 and by February 1920 this appointment had been made full-time at a salary of £85 per annum. Four years later this had risen to £275. Marjorie Postlethwaite joined the staff in 1922 as a young Geography teacher aged 21, straight from Bedford College, at that time described as the London Day Training College. Margaret Richards, joined the staff in 1924 with an impressive clutch of qualifications which included the Cambridge Historical Tripos from Newnham College and a PhD

from London. Her salary was £300 at the time of her appointment. She stayed until 1935 when she left to become Head Mistress of Hove County School. She proved to be a useful contact at the time Selhurst Girls' was evacuated to Hove at the beginning of the Second World War.

Some of the teachers who joined the school as it opened, or as soon as their specialist subject was added to the available curriculum, were still on the staff in 1925 when the first record book of staff appointments was apparently superseded by some other form of record keeping. Miss Lister's foreword in the 1937 School Magazine gave a fulsome appraisal to Miss Nursey when she retired. Interestingly, it seems that Miss Nursey presented the school with several gifts, although there is no mention of what, if anything, was given to her by the School.

The House system was started in 1918, with the houses named after parts of the Empire – Australia, Canada, India and South Africa. Girls were encouraged to participate in House events, with Christmas socials a popular part of the school year. Each girl wore a wooden button as an indication of

which house she was a member. Everyone was encouraged also to do charity work: organised through the House system.

The School Magazines are a particularly good source of information about the development of the school. The first one appears to have been produced in 1925, although the first surviving one is from the following year. The Magazines provide a vibrant and varied account of life at school. They give an excellent insight to the atmosphere prevailing at the time and the

24. Three girls about 1928. The two girls on the right are wearing a uniform, which is not completely standardised, whereas the clothes worn by the girl on the left are completely different.

---

[1] *The gym was housed in the room to be used much later for music.*

25. Girls' Staff about 1925. There were twenty two members of staff and they are believed to be as follows:
Back Row from Left- One, Two and Three are Unknown, Miss Heslop, Miss Rea, Miss Postlethwaite, Miss Harris,
Unknown.
Middle Row from Left: Miss A Smith, Miss Fryer, Miss Moncrieff, Miss Beardsell, Miss Wellman, Miss Jones, Miss
Richards, Unknown.
Front Row from Left: Unknown, Miss Baggs, Miss Moorhouse, Unknown, Mrs Dexter
The unidentified ladies include six of the following seven teachers: Miss Nursey, Miss Gray, Miss Britts, Miss Allen,
Miss Bolton, Miss Chalmers, Miss Collyer, Miss White, Miss K Smith.

time of stress for everyone"

Many of the girls leaving school during the inter-war years went on to higher education and then to become teachers. Selhurst's record of girls obtaining scholarships to Oxbridge at this time was impressive. One of the early editors of the Magazine, Connie Marlow, won an Exhibition to Newnham College, Cambridge from where she wrote to the girls still at school to tell them of her life there. She described the Bachs[sic], Varsity Footlights Club and "indescribably disreputable bicycles."

The Annual Prize-giving was reported with pride in each Magazine. For example, on 11th December 1925 the event opened with bouquets for Miss Wellman and Miss

ethos of the school, which was, from 1922, known as Selhurst Grammar School for Girls. There is both accurate historical detail and partial opinion about events: some events are the parochial ones so beloved of a school community, such as Sports Day or Prize Giving; others are much larger national, or international, issues. The organisation of the editorial committee appears to have been quite inclusive insofar as there was a representative from most of the forms on its Committee, but at the same time it seems to have been lead increasingly

from the top, with the Head Mistress also a member of the Committee.

The General Strike in 1926 was mentioned in the Magazine of that year:

"Many of us were tired, especially the Mistresses, who often had to come long distances by such means as they could devise, all of us were cold, there being no heating in the School, lastly, but not least, the consolation of a hot dinner was denied us. The School is to be congratulated on its good behaviour in a

Leahy, who was to present the prizes and certificates, and a buttonhole for the Chairman of Governors, Captain Stevenson. The latter pointed out that it was the twenty-first Anniversary of the Foundation of the School, and the writer of the report says proudly:

"We were gratified to learn that Selhurst is considered a model school"

A cup had been presented to the school by Alderman Peet to be given each year to the

House which had attained the highest standard of work during that year. There was also a new oak and silver shield to be awarded to the House which had done best in physical exercise. The guest, Miss Leahy, requested an extra day's holiday for the School, which was granted by Miss Wellman. The event closed with the National Anthem and everyone went home contented: either with a prize, a certificate or an extra day's holiday.

Physical exercise was encouraged within the constraints of the era. For the summer of 1925 a new asphalt tennis court was laid and every Thursday at 3.30 two parties of girls set off for the swimming baths at South Norwood: some cyclists, the others pedestrians. There, for an hour, some girls struggled to master different swimming strokes, or how to use the diving boards. The reward for their efforts was simply to be awarded red and white stripes for their bathing costumes as a sign of their "capability and concentration". Even in the 1920s the writer tells us:

"great progress was made, as can be proved by the results of examinations which we are so fond of forming our judgements by…Royal Life Saving 13 elementary certificates, 10 bronze and 5 teacher's certificates"

Edith Wellman retired in 1931. The writer in the School Magazine was effusive in her praise:

"Unwilling to dominate or to impose a rigid discipline, our Head always preferred to lead rather than to drive, and to suggest rather than to enforce. She has brought to her administration of school affairs a kindly wisdom and shrewdness which will long be remembered by the girls and staff who have worked under and with her. Those who know her best appreciate to the full her capacity for understanding others, and her consideration for all who came under her authority"

Her successor was Hannah Lister, another strong leader who also made an enormous contribution to the school's success. Miss Lister was educated at George Watson's College, Edinburgh and Somerville College, Oxford where she read Greats[2]. Her first teaching post had been at Manchester High School where she had been in charge of Classics for thirteen years.

Amongst the many innovations and improvements introduced were included the formation of a School Council at which pupils were able to express their own opinions and suggestions for developments within the school; the modernisation of the Library, thus opening its use to a larger number of pupils; the encouragement of many school clubs and societies, enabling many girls to join in with activities at which they could excel or, at least, they could enjoy. The Fiction Library was removed to the balcony, and the provision of new shelves increased the space available for reference books, of which there were several "valuable additions", including the Encyclopaedia Britannica. It appears that books had hitherto been locked in cupboards, so with the provision of open shelves, girls were being encouraged to use books for studying at school, with older girls also being able to borrow them. This was also:

"a privilege which can be extended to girls lower in the school on the recommendation of a mistress"

In 1933 there appeared a flattering praise of the new school hat bands and badges:

[2] "Greats" - the study of either Classics or Philosophy at Oxford.

"Most visible…are the new school hatbands and badges in school colours of red, gold and black, and our new summer frocks in blue, green and pink which are certainly enlivening the building and field as well as the busy streets of Croydon"

The aspects that are prominent about life at school in this period are the enthusiasm with which all activities appear to have been undertaken, and the great pride with which the pupils treat their membership of the school. There appears to be no false pride or false modesty, simply genuine enthusiasm for all the activities. Obviously, the articles were written either by girls who had enjoyed certain events or who had a particular skill on which to report, but the sentiments expressed seem to have been consistently happy, confident and outward looking, with a charming innocence and ingenuousness.

Sports Day held in 1934, described as "perhaps the most exciting event of our School Year" was described as being held for the first time after a gap of several years. It appeared that from the beginning of June until the day itself on Tuesday July 11th athletic enthusiasts were "practising strenuously". Preliminary heats were held at the end of June and during the early days of July. Invitations and tickets were issued for what was to be a combined Sports and Open Evening. After such preparations it was most disappointing that the rain fell in torrents after the first event had been completed and that the rest of the events had to be postponed until the following Friday morning. The Juniors events included a potato race and blindfold driving, whilst the Seniors performed on flower pots and bicycles. Owing to the postponement the Parents and Staff races were "reluctantly" omitted.

During the course of that same School Year of 1933/34 a Junior Debating Society had

26. Girls' School Assembly Hall. The legend on the post card from which this is copied, describes it as "Croydon Borough School for Girls". This dates it at pre-1922. It should be noted that the balcony, at that time, extended over the area above the stage and would therefore have been around three sides of the School Hall.

been formed. The last debate of its first term was described thus:

"both intellectual and amusing. Five members took the parts of five well-known personalities who were over mid ocean in a ball room [sic], from which, for the safety of others, one had to be thrown. The members were patriotic, for in voting, no-one threw the Prince of Wales out, while several voted for Hitler's rejection, but Amy Johnson was finally cast out as the unlucky one".

A similar debate the following year saw the unfortunate Gordon Selfridge ejected whilst P G Wodehouse, Grace Moore, Anthony Eden and Haile Selassen [sic] managed to remain on board.

During the 1930s several school prospectuses were produced, presumably designed to attract the parents of prospective pupils. Included is a complete list of the current staff of the time – from the Head Mistress right down to the School Keeper- B Hayes of 67 The Crescent, Croydon. The information is attractively presented and clearly expressed: the pride and enthusiasm is most engaging. A great emphasis was placed on effort and dedication, from which results would inevitably flow. Under the heading "General Aims and Organization" it states:

"Based on co-operation rather than rules and regulations…The Head Mistress values the friendly co-operation of parents and is glad to see them as frequently as possible on Tuesday afternoons 2-4, or by arrangement as well as 'At Homes' from time to time"

Unlike the School Magazine which was printed at first by Roffey and Clark and then by F J Lamb at Clapham Junction, the slim

27. Girls' School Laboratory. Again pre-1922, this was the "Chemical Laboratory", neither the furnishings nor the equipment changed much over a period of fifty years!

28. Girls' School Dining Room. Similarly pre-1922, this was in the old dining room, which afterwards became the Library. Note the tablecloths and table decorations, which show an age of greater elegance!

prospectuses of the 1930s were printed almost on the School's doorstep by Geo B Cotton & Co Ltd, The Galleon Press, Sydenham Road, Croydon.

There was much encouragement for girls to become involved in social projects outside school to complement their academic pursuits. One report in the 1935 Magazine is of two weeks spent at the Toddlers' Play Centre in Bloomsbury. Several girls from the 5th and 6th Forms gave up two weeks of their own holidays to go to the centre which provided a month's holiday for "poor children" aged between two and six years. There is a lot of interesting social detail about the arrangements and timetable for each day, and also about the causes of the extreme poverty. Bearing in mind that this was London in the 1930s during a time of mass unemployment, it is especially commendable that girls from a relatively prosperous background were able to witness the plight of others. This is something that shines through from a perusal of what was written at the time: it seems that the girls were being educated not only for the sake of what they could learn in school but also to be able to play a responsible role in a wider society.

A particularly important occasion in the life of the School was the visit by Rear Admiral Hope Harrison and Captain Lethbridge Abell in 1936 to present the ship's bell. A whole host of local dignitaries accompanied them, including the current Mayor of Croydon and

29. This aerial photograph of the school was published as a postcard by Surrey Flying Services in about 1924. Broadway Avenue is on the extreme left, with Edith and Eileen Roads behind the school playing field. Beyond, top left is part of Saxon Road. The Crescent is in the foreground with a large orchard and allotments behind the houses.

several Governors. It had been hanging in the Hall "shrouded in mystery in the shape of a green baize cover". The bell had hung originally in the HMS Woolwich, which was a 'parent ship'[3] to a destroyer during the First World War. The mount had been carved especially by the masters and boys of Stanley Technical School out of wood from the HMS Defiance. Even the bell-rope was interesting, having been made by hand by the caretaker of Stanley School, himself an old sailor. The acquisition of the new bell was a cause of great excitement and, it seems, that Miss Cowell was envied her privilege of ringing it for fire drill!

There appears to be a very strong feeling of a community. For example, when, sadly, one of the girls, Betty Braithwaite, died during the spring of 1936 she was described by Miss Lister as "one of our own". Betty's parents gave the school a beautiful Bible for use at prayers, "in memory of her happy and promising years at Selhurst".

On a happier occasion chairs were arranged in a square shape on the field for a visit by the Premier of New South Wales during July 1936. Half of the seating was reserved for members of the Boys' School. A platform was erected and decorated with jars of flowers and leaves, and also flags. On the right flew a Union Jack, which had been given to the people of Croydon (England) by the people of Croydon (New South Wales) twenty-eight years previously. For the occasion, the Boys sang their School Song and the Girls sang Jerusalem. The Mayor announced that the Premier had asked for the rest of the day to be granted as a holiday, which was greeted with great excitement until it was realised that only three-quarters of an hour remained

---

[3] A provision ship.

of the school day. Fortunately, the following day was a holiday as well.

There were lots of trips organised during this period. Photographs of Versailles, Fontainebleau and French policemen appear as a double page spread in the middle of the 1936 Magazine. A typical girl, the writer reporting the trip which had representatives from five hundred English schools, bemoans the fact that the dormitory for thirty did not have a single mirror. Her description of the French countryside is quite lyrical, although she does remind herself that it was not as beautiful as England! She described seeing oxen drawing a plough – as if they had walked straight out of the Bible. When the group went shopping they were:

> "wildly excited by cute plaid caps and scarves with little men running round the edges, felt wicked riding on escalators and asking if the scarves would wash, but not buying very much."

Even the flower market was exciting as they had to pass animal shops which sold everything from chickens to snakes in bottles.

Many Old Girls kept in touch with their School by sending reports of their activities and further education. To the modern ear some of the reports might sound a little condescending, but there is nevertheless a lot of underlying historical comment, whether it is from the young lady studying Physio-Therapy – a Modern Branch of the Healing Art, or the teacher in Durham – being exposed to a barbarous dialect.

Several gifts were made to the school at this time. The Mayor of Croydon presented a portrait of His Majesty King George VI, Captain Lethbridge Abell gave a silver trophy for House Hockey, a Swimming Cup was presented by the Vth form[4], Miss

Cowell, who was leaving to take up the headship of Southend High School gave a reproduction of Van Gogh's "The Kitchen Garden" and Miss Nursey, one of the founder teachers from 1904, made a presentation of a copy of "Britain and the Beast" upon her retirement.

Four 3rd Form girls were lucky to watch the Coronation Procession on 12th May 1937. Accompanied by Miss Postlethwaite they took their place on Constitution Hill near the Wellington Arch. Amongst other things described in the excitement of the day they describe seeing representatives of the Malay States whose "coffee colour" formed a lasting impression to their innocent eyes.

At this time the building henceforth always "The New Building" was constructed, enabling more gymnastic activity with the provision of two gymnasia, and specialist rooms for both Art and Geography. The effect of this was to release the room formerly used for Art to become a Biology Lab, and to bring Music in from its outside Hut into the room which had been the gym. Unfortunately, the use and enjoyment of such luxury was short-lived with the outbreak of the Second World War.

The foreword in each Magazine written by Miss Lister provides an incisive view of the condition of the school from the top. In 1938 she wrote of the "weeks of international crisis with which the term began" and praises the "spirit of friendliness, co-operation and quiet good sense." Rumours abounded at a classroom level of evacuation to Wales, or Scotland or to the west. Consent forms were taken home to be signed, lists of bare necessities were distributed. Interestingly:

> "we were to be allowed to bring such oddments as young brothers and sisters but the line was drawn at parrots in cages and cats in baskets"

After 1938, the next Magazine was produced in March 1940. By March of that year Miss Lister wrote that they had left for the holidays[5] and when they met again it was to evacuate Selhurst. Some girls described the experience of being evacuated. The walk to Selhurst Station was a walk into the unknown. They did not know where they were going, although it was rumoured that the destination was the Isle of Wight. The pupils actually went to Hove County School for Girls, where the head mistress was a former Selhurst teacher, and they were met with great kindness. It was said that the Hove Staff:

> "even with their own hands carpentered lockers for our books…"

Sharing premises was not easy and the Selhurst girls mainly did their school-work from lunch-time onwards. The Croydon Mayor, Mr Harding visited them in December 1940 and, shortly afterwards, a few of them went home. After Easter the School at Selhurst was re-opened for the junior forms jointly with Selhurst Boys' School. A small group of girls had been evacuated to Bideford[6] where they attended Edgehill College. With July 1940 came the order to leave Hove and the evacuees went to Virginia Water where there was a warm welcome. Unfortunately, whilst it had everything else that could be wished for Virginia Water did not have a suitable building, so the diminishing group went on to Guildford and The Beeches, which soon became a home to them.

The Beeches was built to house a family and a staff of servants, and was not ideal as a school. It was difficult to accommodate Assemblies, but with Miss Lister standing on

---

[4] A number of cups and prizes were acquired during this period.

[5] The summer holidays of 1939.

[6] Bideford was the place to which the Boys' School was evacuated.

a half landing and the girls on two landings and a flight of stairs they were just possible. Lessons were punctuated by the sound of gongs, which had to be used instead of a bell to ensure that nobody outside thought the sound had a more ominous meaning. The surrounding countryside was a source of great delight to many of the evacuated girls whose roots were in a more urban setting. The harebells and other wild flowers reminded them that they were actually on the Hog's Back, and the lawns of the house were of turfs from the Downs. The view of the North Downs was "a joy at any season".

A major concern was to keep the two groups of the school in touch with each other. To this end a scheme was devised for the regular interchange of mistresses. This proved impracticable but visits were made and there was a large amount of correspondence by letter. Miss Lister managed to keep the two halves of the School running smoothly by splitting her time between the two – Selhurst-in-Croydon and Selhurst-at-Guildford.

Still the welfare work continued. At Guildford knitting was done for the evacuated children residing at Court Farm, Hove. Books were collected for the Guernsey children who had been evacuated to Lancashire. In excess of fifty children's garments were made and taken to the Guildford clothes depot for homeless people evacuated from London. Several parcels were sent to the casualty department at Guy's Hospital. An effort was made to respond to Mrs Churchill's appeal for helmets and stockings for the Russian army. In addition, the girls felt an obligation to provide items for the British Army, Navy and Air Force through the Surrey Comforts Fund. Parcels of baby clothes were sent to the Whitehorse Road Crêche and also thirty pairs of socks and mitts were sent to the crew of the MV Clam, the crew of which the school had been in touch with through the Ship Adoption

30. The flying bombs, or doodlebugs, caused a great deal of disruption to school activities during the summer of 1944. The school buildings were badly damaged on several occasions. This photograph shows the front of the Girls' School on the morning of 28th July 1944.

Society.

Meanwhile, during the Easter holidays of 1941, the Croydon Selhurst had also formed a Knitting Group. They too were knitting for the Royal and Merchant Navies, the Army and Air Force, and they made many mittens and sea-boot stockings to send to the Russians allies. Materials were obtained through the Lord Lieutenant of Surrey's Fund. Many enterprising fundraising events were held, including a competition to guess the weight of Sheila Meadowcroft's onion, which raised £2 6s 3d! A special campaign was started to help the National effort for War Savings and during the summer the girls raised £776 18s 4d. The Mayor of Croydon came to set the ball rolling in both the Girls' and Boys' Schools for Croydon's Warship Week and the joint total raised for that was £1,233 0s 6d, an admirable effort.

By 1943 the School had been reunited at Croydon, although during 1944 the staff and pupils had to cope with flying bomb and rockets raids, which could occur at any time of day or night. Lessons often had to take place in air raid shelters or reinforced rooms and corridors.

31. The Boys' School teaching staff in about 1946, with two visitors. The staff are, back row, left to right; B W Harrison; S W Stanswood; A K Walker; A W Ridgewell; E J King; (woman not identified); Miss R V Tickner (School Secretary); H C Hughes; Dr R P R Westgate; G W Hughes: centre row, left to right; E W Swift; P F Holland; R F Egford (almost hidden); two not known; F Mills (almost hidden) J H Taylor: front row, left to right; W M Bennetto; G W Bosustow; H R A Nixon; A J Barlow; F T B Wheeler (Headmaster, standing); Lady guest (unidentified); Mr Ernest Taberner (Town Clerk); W H Stanley; A W Pritchard; J C Wedd; E W King.

THE BOYS' SCHOOL – 1945 to CLOSURE

The Second World War ended in August 1945. Towards the end of the Summer Term, the Headmaster, Mr Turner, had left to take up an administrative post in Wolverhampton. Mr Frederick T B Wheeler M.A. was appointed in his place. He had joined the school staff in 1906. School activities returned more or less to normal and the school sports ground at Waddon was again available for use. The wartime allotments, once described by Mr Wheeler as "plots of cultivated unproductivity" were restored to grass, and lawns again graced the school frontage.

Masters were returning from the forces and temporary staff were leaving. The old dining-room was now inadequate and the handicraft room was converted for dining purposes. Pre-fabricated buildings were put up for handicrafts, and metal work was added to the curriculum. It was 1948 before all the air-raid shelters and blast walls were demolished. The school numbers passed 600, chiefly because of the increasing sixth forms which grew from their pre-war size of twenty to over a hundred. For Higher Schools Certificate, the curriculum allowed

32. The School Library was a popular place for study and reference. The three prefects were photographed there in 1946 and are left to right: R Taverner, G C Gould and M J Pritchard.

33. The sports facilities at The Crescent were inadequate for the need of both girls and boys. For many years the Boys' Sports Ground was at Waddon, seen here with Duppas Hill Road and the Gas Works in the background. Camouflage is just visible on the water cooling towers. This photograph dates from 1941/2 when the sports ground was hardly used because of its close proximity to Croydon Airport. The team is the Rugby 1st XV when there was no 6th form at Croydon. Back Row, left to right are B E W Mansell, Nigel Potts, P W Sadler, Freddie Cole, Alan Meek, J B Selier, R Knott, F Quickenden and Mr E W Swift. Front Row left to right are Bernard Soar, V Searle, Lionel Bishop, Norman Webb, Fred Bailey, Alan Glassington K W Wright.

34. *A view of the assembled schoolboys was familiar to all the staff each morning. No chairs were provided; the boys just sat on the floor or stood at the back, or on the balcony. This photograph dates from about 1946*

choice of four subjects from English, Latin, Greek, French, German, Spanish, History (English and European, Economic and Industrial), Economics, Geography, Statistics and Accountancy, Pure and Applied Mathematics, Physics, Chemistry, Botany, Zoology and Engineering Drawing. In 1950 sixty-nine boys were taking Higher School and the school was winning State Scholarships and many Major and Minor awards. The Senior Athletics Cup of Surrey Grammar Schools was won and music was revolutionised by a new teacher, Mr S.F. Spratt.

The Parents' Association was formed in 1945 and raised useful funds for various school purposes. Speech Days were restored in 1946 and held annually at The Civic Hall until the opening of the Fairfield Halls in 1962.

Mr Wheeler retired at the end of the Summer Term 1950, and Mr Alfred J. Barlow (Second Master) acted as head until the arrival of Mr Charles F.R. Ackland M.A. in January 1951.

Over the next few years a number of the longer-serving members of staff retired. These included Messrs. E W King, G W Bosustow, C W Scott, K M King, A J Barlow, and A W Pritchard.

On 26th September 1954 the school celebrated its 50th anniversary with a service at Croydon Parish Church. The schoolboys walked in procession from Trinity School to the church. Mr C W Scott, by then retired, played the organ and the Bishop of Croydon conducted the service. At the school Speech

35. An Air training Corps was established in 1941 and an early application for the formation of a unit at Selhurst led to 714 Squadron being set up. Messrs Nixon and Mills organised it and within a short time over fifty boys were enrolled. A separate section was formed at Bideford whilst the school was partly evacuated there. Flights from Kenley and summer camps such as this at Lee-on-Solent Naval Air station in 1948 were a popular part of the activities. The participants are, back row, left to right; R W Bustin; E N Hooton; P T Goddard; P W Hoare; A S Clarke (sadly killed later in a gliding accident); Flight Lieutenant H R A Nixon; - Haslar (Naval Officer); Pilot Officer Bennett; ---; D F Goodman; D E Sturdey; D C Riches; Front row, left to right; J B Gent; F H Guyer; D H Ralston; ---; P Smith; - Smith; A Fluck; ---; ---. 714 Squadron eventually became open to non-school members and continued to meet after the closure of the school until their hut was condemned in 2000.

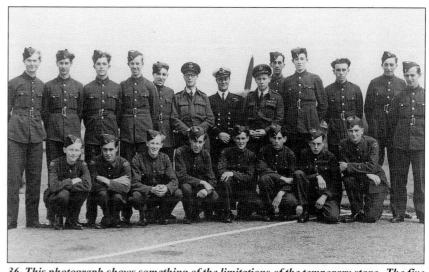

36. This photograph shows something of the limitations of the temporary stage. The five performances of Gilbert and Sullivan's The Mikado, in November 1949 were well-attended. Produced by Mr Pritchard (right as the Mikado, with Katisha – Mrs Hughes), the scenery was painted by Colin Spencer, later to become famous as artist and writer.

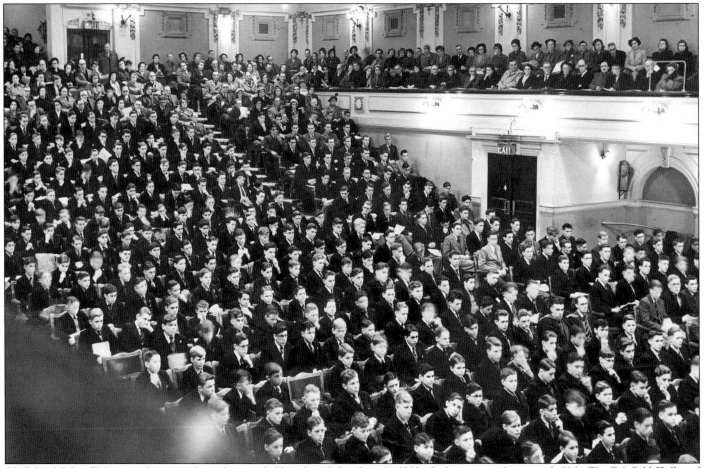

37. School Prize-Giving evenings were in early years held at the Adult School Hall, then in the School Hall and then at The Civic Hall, as seen here in 1952. In later years they were held in The Fairfield Hall, and finally, in the School Hall where they had started.

Day in the Civic Hall on 12th November, the prizes were presented by the Archbishop of Canterbury. It was in 1954 that the school motto, Ludum Ludite, was changed to Semper Recordemur.

By the mid 1950s the post-war baby "bulge" affected the school. In the Autumn Term, 1957 an extra first form was needed and 50 boys had to be accommodated at Whitehorse Junior School for dinners. By the Autumn Term 1959, there were six first forms and nine second forms. These had to be housed at the school's 'new' annexe in the Polytechnic building at Scarbrook Road, under the Deputy Headmaster, Mr J H Taylor. In 1960 there were 15 forms at Scarbrook and 12 at The Crescent. A new science block and dining room opened that year. By the beginning of the Autumn Term 1961, the school had 976 boys on its roll. The Waddon sports ground was replaced by a new one at Auckland Road, South Norwood in about 1965.

Mr Ackland retired at the end of the Spring Term, 1969, and the new Headmaster, Mr Ron A Smith M.A. took over at the start of the Summer Term. By the end of the Autumn Term 1970 there were 605 boys on the roll. Use of the Scarbrook Road annexe had ceased in 1965.

Secondary reorganisation took place in November 1970 and when the school reopened for the Autumn Term on 7th September 1971, it was as Selhurst High School for Boys, the pupils being aged between 14 and 18. There were 633 pupils

38. This photograph was taken in front of the school in the Summer Term of 1951. The staff are, back row, left to right; G A K Plomley; George C Hanmer; J K McKerrow; S F Spratt; R H Squires; J G Povey; A Stewart; Roger O Nebel; Douglas E Honer; Jim Hawkins; C A Winyard: Centre row, left to right; Frank Wells, Charles W Oakley; Philip F Holland; Alan K Walker; S W Stanswood; H R A Nixon; Frank Mills; Joe H Taylor; Hugh C Hughes; W Melville Bennetto; Reg F Egford; A W Ridgewell; Harold E Hore: Front row, left to right; John C Wedd; H A Parkinson; G W Bosustow; C W Scott; Alfred J Barlow; Charles F R Ackland (Headmaster); Miss R V Tickner (School Secretary); Kenneth M King; Ted W King; Alfred W Pritchard; Will H Stanley.

The details of Christian names have been supplied by Douglas Honer who said "we never used first names much and some I never knew". He also explained that for staff photographs they were lined up in order of seniority at the School, the newest members being placed in the back row.

on the roll.

New entrants from Norbury Manor, Ingram and South Norwood schools brought the nominal roll to 732 by the Autumn Term of 1972 but only three of four temporary classrooms had been installed. Since South Norwood was also sending its senior girls to Selhurst Girls', close co-operation and planning was essential between the two Selhursts, Norbury Boys', Norbury Girls', Ingram and South Norwood to ensure continuity of curriculum.

In November 1972 the first of several strikes by staff members of the N.U.T. caused limited teaching on certain days. Ron Smith, Headmaster, recalls that he had to supervise up to 200 boys in the school hall, but could not teach them as that would have been strike-breaking. School prize-givings continued to be held at Fairfield Hall until 1974, when they reverted to the school hall. By 1975 the number of pupils had reached 797, the entry from the three schools being 300 plus each year.

By now the school pupils came from increasingly diverse backgrounds with many pupils of Asiatic and West Indian parentage.

39. A 1960s view in the Handicrafts Workshop

40. The Science Department staff on the day of closure of Selhurst High School for Boys, 22 July 1988. Back row, left to right; Andrew Holmes; Peter Openshaw; Edwin Short (Deputy Headmaster); Geoff Barraclough; Duncan Owen; Andy Andrews; Front row, left to right; Terry Armstrong; Ron Smith (Headmaster); Maggie Davison; Surendra Patel.

A wide range of cultural and religious problems were emerging; assemblies had to cover all the major religions of the world. It was a tribute to the school that no non-Christian parent ever decided to withdraw his son from school assembly (which is a parent's legal right).

Each year entry of 300 was divided into three bands. One aimed mainly at 'O' levels, one aimed at CSEs with a more practical slant. Subjects included all those formerly taught in the Grammar School except Latin and Greek, though music declined through lack of support. Subjects included Technical Drawing, Design, Economics and Social Studies.

Rugby and Cricket continued but with decreasing support, (Rugby was not, in any case, played in the 11 to 14 schools). Football and Athletics flourished, as did Basketball, the school reaching the National Finals one year. New activities included Golf, Tennis, Badminton and Squash.

Societies such as Chess and Debating continued with varying degrees of support, and a Muslim Prayer Group appeared for a while.

By the early 1980s school rolls were falling and meetings were held in 1983/4 to discuss school reorganisations. By 1985 Croydon Council had decided to make the school an annexe of Croydon College. In December 1986 The Selhurst Board of Management was formed as a governing body for the Further Education Centre. On 17th December 1987 the last prize-giving was held in the school hall.

Three school closure parties were held in July 1988 and attended by about 900 former pupils. On 20th July 1988 all the remaining boys, girls and staff of the two schools went to the Isle of Wight and a final luncheon was held on site for all pupils on 22nd July 1988. The schools had served the community for over 80 years but the buildings were destined for a new lease of life.

THE GIRLS' SCHOOL – 1945 to CLOSURE

By December 1945 the School was described as "habitable if not whole". In a building that had been designed for 350 girls, numbers had risen to 560: nearly 70 of whom were in the Sixth Form. Mr Harding retired as Chairman of the Governors. He had been a good friend and was looked upon with great respect, so his retirement was an occasion of regret and sorrow. His support during the War, visiting both Hove and Guildford, was remembered and appreciated. Mrs Dexter also retired in 1945, at the age of 63: she was the last link with the newly opened school of 1904. Described in the early Staff Register as offering Mathematics as a special subject, but also teaching English to Form 1, French Translations in all Forms and as being in charge of the Stationery Stock, she appears to have retired in 1945 as a Latin teacher.

The emphasis on helping those who were less fortunate continued with much enthusiasm and dedication in the period of peace immediately after the Second World War. Selhurst Girls were involved with fund raising for an Inter Schools Fund, formed to help schools in one of the occupied countries. Money was raised from the School Play (£34) and a Sale of Work (£42) even before a country, let alone a school, had been chosen to which the funds were to be directed. A group of girls went as Junior Volunteers to a camp organised by the Berkshire War Agriculture Committee, whereas hitherto they had not camped further afield than Surrey. They worked seven hours a day for the first week:

"pulling charlock from a field of kale. The second week was spent stooking, bean picking and weeding sugar-beet"

During the Easter holidays another group of volunteer Sixth Formers went to Betchworth, Surrey to work at the Waifs and Strays Nursery where they helped to look after twenty two boys and girls aged between 2½ and 5 years.

Annual visits are reported in the School Magazine of visits by 3rd Form girls to Croydon Town Hall which had become regular practice. The first recorded visit appears to have been in 1945 when they were shown round by Mr Berwick Sayers, the Chief Librarian. The trip included a visit to the Police Courts, Council Chamber and Mayor's Parlour. It is almost possible to hear the sigh of relief in the words of the report writer who concludes:

"We did not spend very long in the Reference Library"…

Presumably, it was intended to give the girls both a sense of civic pride and also an insight into the role they could play in their community. After this visit, the Mayor phoned Miss Rea to offer a 15/- certificate for the best written account of the visit. In the end, it seems, two certificates arrived and were shared by four girls.

At this time new staff included the doughty Miss Brown, Maths teacher and later Deputy Head and also Miss Brockwell, whose teaching was directed mainly at girls in the lower forms of the school.

Everything appears to have settled back to normal with relative ease. In 1948 twelve girls had gained University places. Two of those had open exhibitions; the others were all given Croydon major or minor awards to assist with the expense of their further education. The academic successes carried on regularly during this period. Perhaps the apogee was the achievement of Head Girl, Barbara Lloyd who, on the same day in 1957, received offers of places at St Hugh's College, Oxford and Newnham College, Cambridge[1].

The relief of a return to normal life is evident. The enjoyment of the School Sports Day appears to have been pure simple pleasure with the best race that of the mistresses. The writer of the report recorded that nearly all the mistresses, including Miss Lister, took part. It was won by Miss Spark. Even the presentation of the shield was described as a "great occasion" because it had lain hidden away during the War.

In the aftermath of the Second World War and with the growing influence of women in world affairs, the encouragement given to attend Council for Education in World Citizenship meetings was entirely appropriate. From 1948 onwards there are several reports of the meetings. The 1948 meeting was held over a period of four days at Central Hall, Westminster and the main points drawn out by the delegate have a striking importance today:

"To oppose suspicion and fanaticism and the importance of even a little knowledge of languages, and of meeting foreigners as much as possible through travelling and pen friendship."

There were many well-known speakers, including Mr Shinwell, Quintin Hogg, and Rt Hon Sir Hartley Shawcross.

Time was set aside to allow girls to make informed decisions about possible future careers. For example, at different times, they attended talks on Physiotherapy and

---

[1] *It is important to remember that there were fewer Universities at that time, and that places for girls were substantially restricted within the Oxbridge colleges until the 1970s.*

41. Girls' Staff 1960

Back Row from Left: Miss Edmunds (?), Miss Salmon (?) [Latin], Miss Hardy [Geography], Dorothy Bibby [Maths], Unknown, Anna Bissett [German], Jenny Rudge [English], Unknown.

Middle Row from Left: Celia Pearce [Music], Miss Wolfe (?), Shirley Myerscough [Biology], Ann Perry [Biology], Rosemary Hearle [History], Miss Marden [English], Unknown, Miss Postlethwaite [Geography], Mrs Ungar [Latin], Unknown, Chris Gauntlett [English],
Isabel Wilson [Music], Maeve Willis [English], Barbara Brown [Maths], Margaret Freeman [History], Miss Burdess [Art], Vally Reich [German & French].

Front Row from Left: Nora Stapley [History], Miss Brockwell, Mrs Potter [Science], Miss Jones [Chemistry], Miss C I Brown [Maths], Miss Hannah Lister, Miss Slack [PE], Miss Salkeld [French], Miss B Martin [Domestic Science], Miss Henderson [School Secretary], Miss Hutchcroft [French].

Radiography held at Coloma School, another on Social Work at the County School, Guildford and also attended courses which would now be described as Work Experience. One such experience was reported under the title "Life in a University Settlement – an Introduction to Social Work", where the pupil, shortly to start a two year Social Science course at Bedford College, spent three weeks during the summer at this centre in South London, situated in a poor area with a variety of social problems.

Culturally, there was much activity with many visits to the theatre, to concerts and to art exhibitions. During the 53rd season of the Proms in 1948, Miss Wilson took groups of girls to three of the Promenade Concerts, as well as taking others, in the course of the same school year, to the Magic Flute at Covent Garden, to eight different operas (including one at the Davis Theatre in Croydon) and having a season ticket for Robert Mayer's Concerts, of which four were attended at the Central Hall. The annual visits paid by the VIth form to Stratford upon Avon also began that year with a leisurely four day trip. A trip to a Van Gogh Exhibition at the Tate was, by comparison, a very hurried excursion, starting at 9.45 and with the girls returning by bus and tram to be back at school for dinner in the middle of the school day.

Building work in the school brought further changes to the layout. With the completion of two new dining halls downstairs, the room that had hitherto been the dining room became a library, with an attached annexe and three small studies to be used mainly for private music tuition. Two "temporary" prefabs were put up at the side of the playground[2] and the grounds were:

"once more enclosed with neat green railings and the difficulties of playing hockey with half a dozen dogs is a thing of the past[3]"

All the usual clubs and societies continued during this period, although support for Good Causes was arranged in Forms rather than by Houses. The Houses themselves had been renamed. With a diminishing Empire, they were instead given the names of the patron Saints of the British Isles – St. Andrew, St. David, St. George and St. Patrick[4]. At the new French Club, which was at its inception run jointly with the LVI from the Boys' School, only French was to be spoken. This appears to have lead by 1950 to an exchange visit of thirty two girls:

"nous avons reçu la visite d'un certain nombre de jeunes filles de Dunkerque. C'était une visite d'échange."

In March 1960 a further exchange took place, when nineteen girls from Selhurst and four from Coloma, went to Cherbourg, accompanied by Miss Salkeld and Miss Lamont. In return, two months later, they received twenty three girls and two staff from Cherbourg.

There were Ballroom Dancing classes for the older boys and girls, which were, apparently, "attended with enthusiasm". The staff organising these were Miss Brockwell and Mr Wells, whose help was described as "invaluable".

The News Club was a popular School Society[5], where speakers provided information on topical issues. In 1956, a very well-known visitor was welcomed, when Gladys Aylward, the missionary, came to speak to the members. Like many of the speakers, Miss Aylward signed the Minute Book.

Royal occasions were still observed with reverence. On 15th February 1952 the whole School heard the Royal Funeral Service on the radio. The following year, a three-day holiday was granted for the Coronation, when again there were representatives from Selhurst Girls' School along the route. They had an early start and took their positions on the Embankment, where, by 7.45 am, they saw the Navy and Marines marching in to line the route. Later:

"As the golden roof of the State Coach turned the corner of Northumberland Avenue the sun came out.. we had watched a scene that would never be forgotten for the rest of our lives and were all feeling that we should be ever grateful for the opportunity we had to see it as we did".

1954 was a very important year in the history of Selhurst Girls' as it was the occasion of the Silver Jubilee. Starting with the planting of the Jubilee Magnolia on 11th October and continuing for the following fortnight, there were various different celebrations. The whole School filed past to look at the little newly planted tree at the front of the School in a well defined hierarchy – the Governors, Miss Lister, Staff, School Prefects and a representative of each form:

"[the] little tree shook its leaves in the wind and sunshine as much as to say it would do its best to fulfil its part of the hope"

There was a special service of thanksgiving and re-dedication at Croydon Parish Church, when every seat was filled. Obviously a very moving occasion to those who attended, it must also be remembered that it was during a time of post-war optimism, rationing was over, and most people were hoping for a time of prosperity and greater comfort[6]. There were inspiring passages read by Archdeacon Tonks from Ecclesiastes and Ephesians and:

"to the spoken word was added the joyous outburst of hymns of praise, of quiet trust and hopeful vision. The choir made its great contribution to the beauty

---

[2] *At the last time of looking [2003] they were still there.*
[3] *Many railings had been removed throughout Britain as part of the war effort: they were melted down to make into aeroplanes and ammunition.*

[4] *Blue, Yellow, Red, Green respectively*
[5] *It was already in existence by 1945, although the exact year of formation is uncertain.*

[6] *Harold Macmillan claimed in 1957 that Britons had "never had it so good".*

42. Bartered Bride July 1959. Miss Salkeld's production retained the folk-song atmosphere of Smetana's opera. Miss Wilson was Musical Director and the main characters were played by: Christina Brown (Marenka), Cynthia Jones (Jenik), Rita Aps (Marriage Broker), Elizabeth Faulkner (Clown).

of worship in their leading of the hymns, and then the anthem… [the] 1954 generation who were caught, as it were, in the beam of time, and shown as heirs of the past and sponsors of the future"

It is a graceful description of what was obviously seen as a momentous event. There was a Jubilee Fair, which raised almost £400, and an Old Girls' Reunion attended by about 800 Old Girls, many accompanied by their husbands, babies and children. It seems that they came in "relay after relay" from 3 pm to after 10 pm. There was a three tier cake with fifty candles. This was cut by Miss Lister after the husbands and babies had left. She was presented with a "charming travelling clock" – and was described as having to recover from her surprise. There was a further presentation to the retiring Secretary of the Association, Doris Blunt – who was, it seems, delighted, to receive an automatic cookery timer. There were so many guests at this event that, even with the luxury of two dining rooms, supper had to be partaken in two relays.

Throughout the 1950s there was a continuing correspondence with the "Ship". There were various different vessels during this time and a wealth of information about the ships

43. Alderman G J Cole planting the Jubilee magnolia tree in front of the Girls' School on 11th October 1954.

44. Prize Giving: Believed to be 9th November 1960 at the Civic Hall. It was Miss Harley Mason's first Prize Giving as Head Mistress. Guest of honour on that occasion was Dr John Lockwood, Master of Birkbeck College sitting centre, with Miss Lister on his right.

FAIRFIELD HALLS
CROYDON

music is fun

8th, 9th, 10th FEBRUARY
1967

Presented by

POTTERS MUSIC & EDUCATIONAL INSTRUMENTS LTD.

Photo by JON WHITBOURNE

SELHURST GRAMMAR SCHOOL FOR GIRLS' ORCHESTRA

45. Music is Fun. This depicts the Selhurst Girls' Orchestra on stage at the Fairfield Halls in 1967 for a competition organised for Surrey school orchestras. The orchestra progressed to the final in which they were placed second to the eventual winners: Wallington County Grammar School for Girls. Standing on the extreme right of the photograph is the redoubtable Mrs P E Norman, Music Teacher.

themselves, their crews and the places to which they travelled, but more particularly their reasons for the various voyages, some political, some social: the constraints of this booklet are such that it is not possible to do justice to this topic.

Whilst discipline within the School was rigorously enforced, with strict penalties for minor misdemeanours, there was less external regulation from central or local government. At times, the Head Mistress awarded "occasional holidays". Half term holidays were not so structured as they subsequently became, which enabled greater flexibility in the awarding of these extra days. Princess Margaret's Wedding in 1960 was such an occasion, but by the Investiture of the Prince of Wales in 1969, it is suggested that most of the School watched the ceremony on television. As there was, at that time, only one television, in one ordinary classroom, this might be an exaggerated suggestion!

The first record of a Joint Commemoration Service at Croydon Parish Church appears in 1955. The inauguration of this event was encouraged and supported by Archdeacon Tonks, Governor of the School and Vicar of Croydon. By 1963 the Service had to be split into two, as the number of pupils was too great to be accommodated together: the size of the Boys' School had increased substantially, owing to the large intake of the post-war "bulge" in 1958.

The annual Prize Giving had been held for many years at the Civic Hall in Croydon[7], and then developed into a grand occasion at the Fairfield Halls. In 1968 it was no longer possible to hire the Fairfield Hall, so Prize Giving was held in the School Hall, split into Junior and Senior occasions, in order to accommodate guests.

By 1959, when Miss Fryer retired after 41 years as the PE teacher and 1960, when Miss Lister retired after 29 years, times were changing. Croydon became a London Borough in 1965 at which time the Borough's coat of arms changed from that depicted on the Selhurst Girls' School badge. There were many meetings and consultations concerning the future of education in Croydon. This lead inexorably to the system which was introduced in 1971 when the Grammar, Secondary Modern and Technical Schools ceased to exist and were renamed and reorganised as High Schools.

There were many presentations to Miss Lister at her retirement, not least a book which was compiled by all the girls and later returned to the School after her death on 5th November 1974. Miss Lister had a long and distinguished career as a Head Mistress: she was President of the Association of Head Mistresses from 1952-54. She had helped to compile a book published by that Association to celebrate its centenary in 1974. To Miss Lister fell the task of writing various obituaries for former members of staff for School Magazines. In 1961 Misses Amy Smith (1913-45) Hannah Bennett (1933-1959) and Margaret Richards (1923-1934) died and she wrote about them all. Throughout her retirement she visited Selhurst regularly and she was, it seems, thrilled with the newly opened Skills Centre[8] and the method and approach of teaching English to immigrants to Britain. Appropriately, a Service of Thanksgiving for her life was held at Selhurst in June 1975.

Miss Lister's successor as the fourth Head Mistress of Selhurst Girls was Miss Harley Mason, to whom fell the task of all the preparatory work for the changes to comprehensive education. As a member of the Working Party on the Reorganisation of Secondary Education in Croydon, the Head Mistress was required to attend numerous meetings at the Education Office. In 1969 Miss Harley Mason was the first Head Mistress of Selhurst Girls who left, not to retire, but to move to another school and her successor was Mrs B E Green[9] who lead the school through the transition from Grammar to High School in 1971. Life in the classroom continued as before and the education received by the girls who joined the school during this period was as academically challenging as previously, but

society itself changed during the 1960s. Fund raising for "good causes" continued with enthusiasm. In 1961 there were collections in Assembly for Congo Famine Relief, for the Oxford Committee for Famine Relief and for the Peckham Settlement. Two years later, nearly £500 was raised for the Freedom from Hunger Campaign, when an Autumn Fair was held, and from collections in Assembly. The last big event during this period was held in support of the Save the Children Fund in December 1967, when £320 was raised at an evening Fair opened by Mr Jerome Willis, actor brother of Miss Maeve Willis, then head of the English Department.

Academic successes continued. In 1963, for example, Mary Skinner was offered an Open Award to the London School of Economics to read Economics and Computational Methods, and Dianne Bulgen gained an Elizabeth Garrett Anderson Scholarship to the Royal Free Hospital School of Medicine. As further education expanded, a larger number of girls were able to take the opportunities offered.

In 1965 there were several retirements of staff who had given long service to the School. Miss Henderson retired after thirty-one years as School Secretary. School Secretaries appear, in fact, to have been traditionally long-serving, as the previous one, Miss Lawrence, who retired in about 1932 had been twenty two years in her post. Two School Secretaries covering a period of fifty-three years was a remarkable achievement. Miss Salkeld retired after twenty-eight years in Modern Languages and Miss Wilson after twenty-three years in Music.

Sport continued to be popular with a core group of girls. Each year there were Hockey and Netball teams competing against other local schools in the winter; similarly Tennis, Rounders and Athletics teams in the summer term. Also, there were individual successes

[7] Often referred to as "The North End Hall", its original name, in reports of the event.

[8] 1974.
[9] Esmé Green.

46. Library – formerly Dining Room before construction of New Building.

47. Class in session – Biology Lab, former Art Room, believed to be 1958/59.

for girls and teams at other events, such as the Badminton Team who had a notable success in 1966 by winning the Surrey Schools' Badminton Association Tournament and returned proudly with a silver cup which was displayed in the trophy cabinet on the school balcony for a whole year; or the Trampolining Team who won the Croydon Schools Championship in 1969; or Maureen Gant who dived for Great Britain. These teams and girls were encouraged and supported by Miss Lowther[10] who had joined the staff in 1960 and stayed until the School finally closed.

Just before the change of name to Selhurst High School for Girls in 1971, Miss Brown retired. Feared by many for her sharp comments and all-seeing eyes, she represented the end of an era. She was the last of the teachers who had experienced any of the hardship of wartime Selhurst. Her companion Pekinese, Nanki Poo, who came to school with her several times a week, terrorised many girls whose ankles were at risk during Maths lessons.

The last intake of approximately ninety eleven-year-old girls was admitted in the autumn of 1970. Selhurst High School for Girls was designated as a school for 14-18 year olds. In 1971, approximately one hundred and forty girls, the equivalent of about six classes, were admitted into the Fourth Year from the feeder schools of Norbury Manor and South Norwood High Schools. They were split into mixed ability groups with the existing three Grammar School classes of that year group. Immediately there was an accommodation problem, as no new buildings had been completed: even the temporary new

---

[10] *latterly Mrs Todd..*

classrooms were not ready.[11]   The girls themselves were physically bigger, being three years older than previous new entrants. The Sixth Form at that time, who were being taught in smaller "A" Level groups, found themselves being taught in some very strange locations. There were French classes taking place grouped round the wash basins at the end of a cloakroom, whilst some RE lessons were held in the front room of one of the students who, quite conveniently, happened to live in The Crescent.

Mrs Green retired prematurely from the Headship in 1982 owing to ill health, leaving Margaret Freeman as Acting Head. Miss Freeman joined the School in 1954 as a History teacher and had been Deputy Head since Miss Brown's retirement in 1971. The final Head Teacher was Dr David Dibbs from 1984-87 but the task of seeing the School through to closure fell to Miss Freeman, as Dr Dibbs had already moved to another School a year before Selhurst Girls was due to close.

With the change of name, had also come changes to the curriculum. Social Studies and Commerce were added.[12] Throughout the 1970s admission numbers had remained quite constant with up to three hundred girls joining the School each year, but after that numbers began to fall substantially and by 1985 had dropped so low that closure became inevitable. On June 28th 1986 there was a party held in the Girls' School to mark the first stage in the School's closure. Many former members of staff and pupils attended the event. From 1986/87 Year there was a Sixth Form Centre run in conjunction with Selhurst Boys' School and the doors of Selhurst Girls' School finally closed in 1988.

---

[11] In 1972 a national strike of Building Workers caused further delays to the erection of the new Sixth Form block.

[12] Commerce had been provided for a while during the period c.1916.

48. Margaret Freeman and Ron Smith cut the cake at closure in 1988.

SUBSEQUENT EVENTS – 1988 to 2004

After closure at the end of the Summer Term, 1988, the Boys' School premises became an annexe to Croydon College as a centre for further education. The Girls' School premises became the BRIT School for the performing arts and technology.

Croydon College was incorporated as an independent company in April 1993 and became owner their part of the property. The college very soon notified Croydon Council that it wished to cease using the premises by September 1997. Meanwhile Ingram School had severe problems. In 1995 it had been inspected by Ofsted and placed on special measures. However it was making little progress and the premises in Thornton Heath were considered outdated and unsuitable for improvement. The Ingram Governors expressed an interest in transferring to the Selhurst site, but Croydon Council had first to buy it back from Croydon College. Eventually agreement was reached and the premises were bought back at council tax payers' expense for over 2½ million pounds. However this arrangement did avoid even greater expenditure on the Ingram site.

The Governing body of Ingram Boys' High School wished the name to be changed and when the school transferred to Selhurst at the start of the Autumn Term 1997, it became again, Selhurst High School for Boys, teaching 11 to 16 year olds.

SELHURST HIGH SCHOOL for BOYS 1997 to 2004

For some years a proportion of the intake of pupils at Selhurst had come from Ingram School. The first few years of the new school at Selhurst were very difficult. However in 1999 Mrs Joan Pickering was appointed Head Teacher and the school came out of special measures by June 2000, receiving a DfES School Improvement Award in the same year. With a good team she succeeded in obtaining a positive Ofsted Report by 2002. Selhurst is now an Excellence in Cities School and gained Sportsmark Award in 2003. Improvements have included the introduction of a school council, the installation of three computer suites, and the introduction of a new school uniform. The school is bidding for Specialist College Status and a new flood-lit all-weather pitch and outdoor facilities have been installed. It is hoped to provide additional sports and ICT facilities.

The curriculum now includes English, Mathematics, Science, Humanities (History, Geography and Religious Studies), Art, Modern languages (French and Spanish), Design Information, Food Technology, Physical Education, Drama, Music and PSHE (Personal, Social and Health Education) including Citizenship. For older pupils there are additional opportunities with Business Studies, Drama, Music and Sociology. All pupils take part in two weeks Work Experience towards the end of their schooling. There is a wide range of sporting activities including Football, Rugby, Flag Football, Basketball, Cricket and Athletics. School journeys are arranged, both abroad and nearer home. There is a Gospel Choir and Steel Drums Workshop and a flourishing Art department. Regular theatre visits are organised by the Drama department and an Aim Higher project enables boys to raise their aspirations for Higher education.

THE BRIT SCHOOL for the PERFORMING ARTS & TECHNOLOGY

This now occupies the former Girls' School premises having opened in 1991. A splendid new building was erected on the field behind. The BRIT School is an independent state funded City College for the Technology of the Arts. It is the only one of its kind dedicated to education and vocational training for the Performing Arts, Media, Visual Arts and Design, and the Technologies that make performance possible. It is a school for 14-19 year olds and has a unique and pioneering approach to education.

BRIT stands for the British Record Industry Trust which is the school's sponsor. Under its principal, Nick Williams, the school provides specialist arts training as well as a very good general education, encouraging students to go on to specialist colleges and universities or into employment in the creative industries. Its examination performance in the Arts and National Curriculum has placed it among the best achieving schools in the country. It accepts students from most of Greater London and parts of Kent and Surrey and usually caters for about 800 at any one time. Her Majesty the Queen visited the school as part of the Golden Jubilee Celebration in 2003.

THE OLD CROYDONIANS' ASSOCIATION

Football matches between the School and the Old Boys commenced in 1909 and the School's annual athletic meetings included Old Boys' events. In Autumn 1910 an "Old Boys" Section was included in the School Magazine, "The Croydonian". A dinner was held at the Café Royal, Croydon on 11th November 1911 following the annual football match between the Old Boys and the School and the Old Croydonians' Association was born. The first General Meeting of the Association was held on 31st March 1912, the Headmaster, Mr Arthur Hillyer, being unanimously elected as the first President. The annual subscription was 2/6d, but Country Members, living more than fifteen miles away paid only 1/-. Social events in the early days included an Annual Dinner, smoking concerts, and whist drives. The first sports sub-section of the Association was a Swimming Club, sponsored by Mr F T B Wheeler in 1913. Ties and hat bands in the Association colours made their first appearance in the same year. When the School moved to The Crescent, the School Governors gave permission for the new building to be the headquarters of the Association. A Gymnasium Class and Rambling and Cycling sections were formed but the war halted further developments and activities were suspended.

The Association resumed meeting soon after the war. The Cricket Club started in the summer of 1922 and the Football Club in the winter of 1922/23. In 1925 the School and the Association changed over to playing Rugby. At various times Gymnastics, Swimming, Harriers, Badminton, and Tennis enjoyed some degree of support. In 1931 an Old Boys' Masonic Lodge was formed. The Surrey Arts and Sciences Lodge, No.5310 continues but is now open to non-school members.

The Rugby Club leased a ground at Elmers End in 1926/27 but for some time the Association made determined efforts to obtain its own Sports Ground. Success was achieved in 1934 when a pavilion and

49. The Old Croydonians' Association celebrated its 50th Anniversary in 1961 with a Jubilee Dinner at the Shirley Park Hotel.

Old Croydonians' Association

JUBILEE DINNER

SHIRLEY PARK HOTEL
CROYDON

Saturday, 11th Nov., 1961

Chairman:
C. F. R. ACKLAND, Esq., T.D.

MENU

Cream of Mushroom Soup Cara Nutrix

Grilled Fillet Sole Scarbrook

Roast Norfolk Turkey Jubilee—Chipolata
Croquette Potatoes
Buttered Runner Beans

Pear Belle Helene

Coffee

TOAST LIST

"THE QUEEN"
Proposed by - - - THE CHAIRMAN

"THE ASSOCIATION"
Proposed by - - - G. RATCLIFFE, Esq.
Response by - - - W. E. AUSTIN, Esq.

"THE GUESTS"
Proposed by - - - J. A. HUNSWORTH, Esq.
Response by - - - Coun. E. J. FOWLER

"THE CHAIRMAN"
Proposed by - - - J. B. KANE, Esq.

ground in Purley Way was leased from the Air Ministry. The threat of war in 1938 led to its requisition. Croydon Corporation provided accommodation on the playing fields opposite the aerodrome for the 1938/39 season but games then ceased for the war years.

Most other activities were suspended but newsletters were published up to 15 times a year. By 1946 circulation had reached 700. A War Memorial Fund was set up to commemorate those Old Boys who fell during the war. The Association Council felt it would be ideal to obtain a new sports ground. Meanwhile a Roll of Honour was compiled. A War Memorial was designed by Mr H C Wilkinson, Art Master, and was constructed in the school workshop under the supervision of Messsrs R O Nebel and J McKerrow. (illustration 51 on page 47). A Book of Remembrance was published in 1949.

The Rugby Club resumed playing for the 1946/7 season, temporarily at Twickenham. The club were back at Addington for the 1947/48 season and at Purley Way for the 1950/51 season. After much searching a ground was purchased in 1965 in Layhams Road, near New Addington, just beyond the Croydon boundary. Funds had to be raised and the late Dudley Spice approached OCA members, issuing loan notes. Because the Department of Education and Science would only grant funds to non-incorporated "open" clubs it was necessary to allow non-Old Boys to join. The Old Croydonians Sports Club was born and a 50% government grant was received. The Association made a substantial loan.

When the ground opened in 1970 there were two rugby pitches and a cricket pitch, but very soon cricket could not be played there due to the high cost of maintenance. Changes at the school and its eventual closure meant that recruitment for the Rugby Club was much reduced. The playing members were ageing, and the change of name to Croydon RFC barely improved matters. The freehold of the ground was sold to the Sports Club in 1988. The Rugby Club was disbanded and the ground was sold in December 2003.

Unfortunately it has not been possible to trace any records of the Old Girls' Association. As early as 1928, however, the School Magazine included reports from Old Girls such as a description of teaching country children a long way from home: the writer was twenty six miles from Croydon! In a 1934 report of the Christmas Reunion it is stated that the Club "meets three times a year and has Dramatic and Badminton sections". The subscription, at that time, was 2/- a year or 10/6d for life. Correspondence from abroad continued for as long as the School Magazine was published. It is not clear, however, whether many of these correspondents were members of the Old Girls Association, or simply Old Girls of the School. It is thought that The Association ceased to exist in the late 1970s.

50. Girls' Reunion c 1954 – for the Jubilee. This took place in both dining rooms, although the one depicted here is the Front one. It should be noted that there are men and children as well as Old Girls!

51. The Second World War Memorial Lectern in the Boys' School Hall was in the "care" of Croydon Education Department when the School closed in 1988. Unfortunately, it has not been seen since.

The Old Croydonians' Association had gone through some difficult years from the 1950s as membership declined and few new members joined. It is invidious to mention names as so many people have worked hard over the years on behalf of the Association, but without the efforts of stalwarts such as George Ratcliffe, Eric Austin, Ray Carter and Bernard Woolnough it would no doubt have closed.

In 1983 it was recorded that there had been no committee meetings of the Girls' Association for at least three years, and that it had folded. A Special General Meeting of the Old Croydonians' Association was held on 8th March 1984 when revised rules were agreed permitting girls to join. The first one did not do so until 1991 and girls first attended a reunion in 1993. Since then the valiant efforts of Dick Etherington in tracking down former pupils from both schools, has led to a greatly increased membership and attendance at functions. Sadly, he can no longer attend meetings for health reasons but the Association owes him a great debt of gratitude. Meanwhile, the Old Croydonians' Association appreciates the support of its President, Ron Smith M.A., and its Vice-President, Joan Pickering M.A.

52. Following interior alterations to the Boys' School Hall the Old Croydonians Association in 2003 funded the repositioning of the war memorials to the school entrance hall. A small wooden plaque has replaced the lost lectern (above). The Head Teacher, Joan Pickering is seen here with the memorials and some of the boys. The memorials record the names of 171 former pupils and two members of staff who were known to have lost their lives in the two World Wars.

A good relationship has been established with the BRIT School and with Selhurst High School for Boys, it is hoped that new younger members will join so that the Association can continue for many years to come.

SOURCES and ACKNOWLEDGEMENTS

The information in this book has been obtained from a number of sources. The following publications have been invaluable:

The Selhurst Book 1904-1925

Selhurst Grammar School for Boys 1904-1954

A Book of Remembrance 1949

The Old Croydonians' Association 1911-1936

The Croydonian (School Magazine) 1906 – 1980s

The Old Croydonian (OCA Magazine)

The School Magazine - Selhurst Grammar School for Girls

The following unpublished sources housed in Croydon Local Studies Library:

School Log Books *

School Admission Registers

Croydon Education Committee Minutes

* available for reference only by special permission

The following people have given a great deal of assistance. The Editors and the Association appreciate their help:

The staff of Croydon Local Studies Library, especially Chris Bennett (Archivist) and Steve Roud (Local Studies Librarian).

Ray Carter, Marjorie Chandler, Margaret Freeman, Douglas Honer, Ron Smith, Yvonne Woodley, Bernard Woolnough, Tony Yeoell.

ILLUSTRATIONS

Croydon Local Studies Library:	Nos. 1, 3, 10, 14, 15, 16, 17, 18, 20, 22, 23, 24, 25, 30, 31, 32, 33, 34, 37, 38, 39, 41, 42, 43, 44, 45, 46, 47, 50, 51.
John Gent Collection:	Nos. 2, 4, 5, 6, 7, 8, 9, 11, 12, 13, 26, 27, 28, 29, 35, 36 (Tony Hanscombe), 49, Cover, Inside Front Cover
Ron Smith:	Nos. 40, 48
The Selhurst Book:	Nos. 19, 21.
Tom Nicholls:	Nos. 52, Inside Back Cover.